BIG MAMA WISDOM FOR COUPLES

205 Questions to Ask & Discuss Before Marriage

CYNTHIA KNIGHT

Second Edition Revised

Onyx Gavel Publishing • Baltimore, Maryland

BIG MAMA WISDOM FOR COUPLES Second Edition

Copyright © 2012, 2021 by CYNTHIA KNIGHT

Cover Designer: RebeccaCovers

Interior Layout Designer : Nasim M. Sarkar

All rights reserved. No part of this book may be reproduced or transmitted in any form or by any means without written permission from the author.

ISBN 978-0-9852542-3-0 First Printing 2012

ISBN 978-0-9852542-6-1 Second Printing 2021, revised

Printed in the United States of America

Published in USA by Onyx Gavel Publishing

A subsidiary of Mosaic Consortium Group, LLC.
www.onyxgavel.com

publish@onyxgavel.com

Dedication

This book is dedicated to my firstborn, Christina "Teenie-Weenie" Knight, and my family, the core of my inspiration. You challenge me to keep going every day. I love you.

Contents

Introduction 1
Big Mama Wisdom Key 2
The Basics 3
Career & Finances 36
Religion & Spirituality 76
Sex & Intimacy 94
Family Life 120
Generational Issues 146
Social Media 154
House & Home 174
Personal Issues 188
References 220
About The Author 221

Introduction

"Mom, I'm getting married," my eighteen-year-old daughter said to me. "Eventually," I said casually. "No, I'm getting married next year." A flood of emotions and questions ran through my mind. What came out of my mouth next was, "You know nothing about this guy." Then I started belting out questions to prove I knew that she didn't know enough about her Boyfriend to get married, hence the birth of this book.

A famous comedian once said, "Big Mama is gone." But the frank and wise advice from our Big Mama lives on in the memories of many. Some threw away the wisdom of Big Mama as old-fashioned and out of date, and some of us kept it close and cherished it, like the old family Bible. This Mama knew her daughter wasn't ready for marriage—the relationship didn't even survive the printing of this book.

Sometimes the freshness and newness of love and romance cloud the thinking of the love-struck. Couples neglect to think about the seriousness of the lifelong covenant bond they are about to embark on with another individual. Couples should discuss everything from basic questions to generational issues before considering marriage.

This book is meant to aid in sparking those numerous conversations that need to take place before any couple walks down the aisle. Not every question will be a serious one. Some are just a matter of personal preference, but it's important to note that personal preference can be a deal-breaker in a relationship. Big Mama Wisdom for Couples cannot address every topic, but I hope this book will cover some of the crucial questions that Big Mama would want you to ask.

~Enjoy!

Big Mama Wisdom Key

This is a red-flag question and, depending on the answer, should spark some concern. Big Mama would advise, "Proceed with caution and listen more than you talk." Be sure to ask follow-up questions until you are satisfied that you understand what was explained to you.

This is a question that may provoke an answer which requires further investigation. You may decide you need more information. Don't be afraid to look deeper; in fact, Big Mama strongly suggests you look deeper into the matter. Follow your instincts.

Big Mama would never judge ... but she gives her advice freely. In this instance she says, "Run!" Don't say you weren't warned.

BMW
Big Mama's thoughts on a matter—the proverbial period at the end of a sentence.

The Basics

The basic questions are fundamental questions for any developing relationship, platonic or romantic. If you are unsure of any of the answers to "the basics," Big Mama strongly recommends spending more time getting to know the individual you are contemplating marrying.

QUESTION #1

What do you do for a living?

Notes

QUESTION #2

What are your hobbies?

Notes

QUESTION #3

What motivates you?

Notes

QUESTION #4

What do you like to do in your spare time?

Notes

QUESTION #5

Are you a stay-at-home person or a social person?

Notes

QUESTION #6

What social clubs/ activities do you actively participate in?

Notes
_____
_____
_____
_____
_____
_____
_____

QUESTION #7

Do you participate in social networking?

Notes

QUESTION #8

What are your pet peeves?

Notes

QUESTION #9

Do you smoke?

Notes

QUESTION #10

Do you drink?

Notes

QUESTION #11

Do you like to travel?

Notes

QUESTION #12

What is your political affiliation or party of choice?

Notes
_____
_____
_____
_____
_____
_____

QUESTION #13

What helped shape your current political viewpoint?

Notes

QUESTION #14

Are you a sports fan?

Notes

QUESTION #15

> *How important is physical fitness to you?*

Notes

QUESTION #16

What is your favorite color?

Notes

QUESTION #17

What is your favorite type of flower?

Notes

QUESTION #18

What is your favorite flavor of ice cream?

Notes

QUESTION #19

What is your favorite type of music?

Notes

QUESTION #20

What is your favorite movie?

Notes

QUESTION #21

If you could only listen to one song for the rest of your life, what would it be?

Notes

QUESTION #22

What movie could you watch over and over and over and never get tired of it?

Notes

_____
_____
_____
_____
_____
_____

QUESTION #23

What is your guilty pleasure?

Notes

QUESTION #24

When you are having a bad day, what makes you feel better?

Notes

QUESTION #25

Would you describe yourself as an introvert or an extrovert?

Notes

QUESTION #26

Do you have a best friend that is of the opposite sex?

Notes

QUESTION #27

Do you believe men and women can be in purely platonic relationships?

Notes
....
....
....
....
....
....

QUESTION #28

What is your fondest memory?

Notes

QUESTION #29

If you could, what is the one thing that you would change about yourself?

Notes

QUESTION #30

What does a healthy relationship look like to you?

Notes

QUESTION #31

What should I know that I'd never think to ask about you?

Notes

Career & Finances

Finances and career choices are typically a challenge for any couple. The questions that follow are intended for couples who are engaged or planning to combine households. They are not in any particular order. They are random questions that cover a variety of topics, with the hope of generating candid conversation.

QUESTION #32

Are you currently employed?

Notes

QUESTION #33

What are your long-term career goals?

Notes

QUESTION #34

What is your credit score?

Notes

QUESTION #35

Are you coming into the relationship with existing debt?

Follow-Up: If so, How much?

Notes

QUESTION #36

> **Do you have a plan to manage any existing debt you may have?**

Notes

QUESTION #37

Are you open to financial planning?

Notes

QUESTION #38

Do you have any student loans?

Follow-Up: Approximately how much do you owe?

Notes

QUESTION #39

Do you feel you know how to manage money?

Notes

QUESTION #40

If you applied for a mortgage or a loan today, would you get approved?

Notes

QUESTION #41

Are you finished with your education?

Notes

QUESTION #42

Do you anticipate taking on additional educational debt in the next five years?

Notes

QUESTION #43

Have you ever been fired from a job?

Notes

QUESTION #44

Are we going to keep our money together or separate?

Notes

QUESTION #45

In the marriage, who is going to pay the bills?

Notes

QUESTION #46

Will the responsibility of the bills be divided, or assigned to one person?

Notes

QUESTION #47

How do you plan to support the family?

BMW: There should be a plan ... just saying.

Notes

QUESTION #48

How do you expect to be supported?

Notes
___
___
___
___
___
___

QUESTION #49

What type of lifestyle do you expect to live?

BMW: Your answers should be very similar to avoid problems in the future.

Notes

QUESTION #50

Do you owe any back taxes?

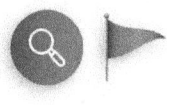

Notes

QUESTION #51

How much money do you spend on your sports or hobbies?

Notes

QUESTION #52

How many jobs have you had in the last five years?

Notes

QUESTION #53

Do you owe/pay alimony or child support payments?

Notes

QUESTION #54

How many credit cards do you have?

Notes

QUESTION #55

Do you pay your bills on time?

Notes

QUESTION #56

Do you have any liens?

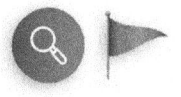

Notes

QUESTION #57

How do you handle your personal finances?

Notes

QUESTION #58

Do you expect to share a joint bank account?

Notes

QUESTION #59

Do you believe in Pre-nuptial agreements?

Notes

QUESTION #60

Do you expect a pre-nuptial agreement?

Notes

QUESTION #61

Would you be open to a post-nuptial agreement?

Notes

QUESTION #62

How important is your career?

Notes

QUESTION #63

Do you have a savings account?

Notes

QUESTION #64

Do you own any property?

Notes

QUESTION #65

Do you travel on your job?

Follow-Up: How much time do you spend away from home on average?

Notes

QUESTION #66

Is there anything in your past that would prevent you from getting a security clearance?

Notes

QUESTION #67

Do you gamble?

Notes

QUESTION #68

Are you a care-free spender?

Notes

QUESTION #69

Do you live by a budget?

Notes

QUESTION #70

If you went on a shopping spree, how much money would you typically spend?

Notes

Religion & Spirituality

From Big Mama's standpoint this is the most important topic. Couples must discuss and agree on this area before the wedding. This crosses over every aspect of your life, from your personal beliefs to children, family, and ceremony. Just for the record, Big Mama is a God-fearing, Bible-toting, church-going, Holy-Ghost-filled Christian.

QUESTION #71

What are your views on religion and spirituality?

BMW: You need to be on the same page here from the beginning ... equally yoked.

Notes

QUESTION #72

Do you believe in God?

Notes

QUESTION #73

> *What is your religious affiliation and/or denomination?*

BMW: Beware of cults.

Notes

QUESTION #74

Do you go to church?

Notes

QUESTION #75

Do you attend church regularly (i.e. weeknights, every Sunday)?

Notes

QUESTION #76

Do you read the Bible?

Follow-Up: Do you read the Koran or any other religious book?

Notes

QUESTION #77

Do you believe in Heaven and Hell?

BMW: Whether you believe it or not does not impact the fact that they both exist ... just saying.

Notes

QUESTION #78

> *Are your lifestyle and daily behavior governed by your religious beliefs?*

Notes

QUESTION #79

What religious faith do you expect your children to be raised under?

Notes

QUESTION #80

How important is it to you that your children have a religious background?

Notes

QUESTION #81

How important is God in your life?

Notes

QUESTION #82

Do you have any relatives/friends who practice witchcraft, voodoo, or the occult?

BMW: Birds of a feather flock together...

Notes

QUESTION #83

Do you practice witchcraft, voodoo or the occult?

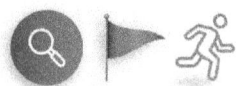

Notes

QUESTION #84

How important a role will religion/spirituality play in our relationship?

Notes

QUESTION #85

Do you have a personal relationship with God?

Notes

QUESTION #86

How much of your faith would you want to incorporate in the wedding ceremony?

Notes

Sex & Intimacy

The sex and intimacy questions are fundamental questions necessary for developing a healthy and mutually satisfying sexual relationship. The questions focus on the discovery of information regarding past and future practices, thoughts, and viewpoints. Please use these questions as a catalyst for more in-depth conversations. Big Mama is not a prude.

QUESTION #87

How do you define romance?

Notes

QUESTION #88

How do you define intimacy?

Notes

QUESTION #89

What is your love language?

Notes

QUESTION #90

What do you consider a romantic evening?

Notes

QUESTION #91

Do you believe in monogamy?

Notes

QUESTION #92

Are you polyamorous?

BMW: If this is not your lifestyle....stay away

Notes

QUESTION #93

Do you believe in sex before marriage?

Notes

QUESTION #94

Are you currently practicing celibacy?

Notes

QUESTION #95

What went wrong in your prior relationships?

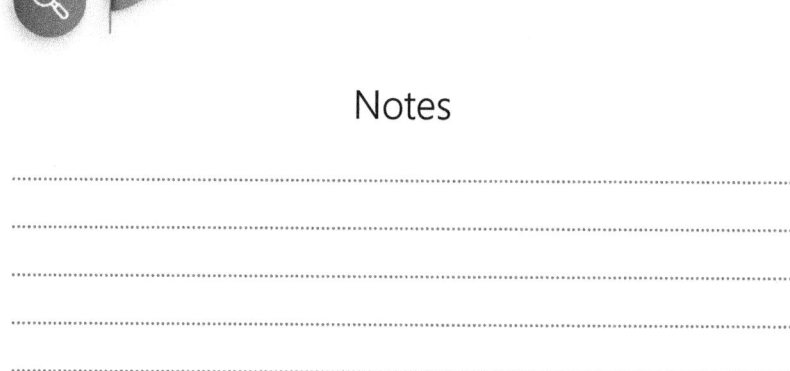

Notes

QUESTION #96

Have you ever cheated in your past relationships?

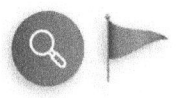

Notes

QUESTION #97

How important are truth and honesty in a relationship to you?

Notes

QUESTION #98

Do you feel it is okay to lie and/or keep secrets in a relationship?

Notes

QUESTION #99

What is your relationship "deal breaker"?

Notes

QUESTION #100

Are you open to couples therapy? Pre-marital counseling? Post-marital counseling?

Notes

QUESTION #101

How do you like to resolve disagreements/arguments?

Notes

QUESTION #102

How often do you like/ expect to have sex?

Notes

QUESTION #103

Have you ever participated in alternative sexual relations (i.e., ménage à trois, partner swapping)?

BMW: If this is not your lifestyle...stay away.

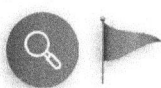

Notes

QUESTION #104

Have you ever participated in a bisexual/homosexual relationship?

BMW: If this is not your lifestyle...stay away.

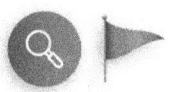

Notes

QUESTION #105

What is your sexuality?

(heterosexual, bisexual, homosexual, other)

BMW: Your answers should match!

Notes

QUESTION #106

Are you a transgender individual?

Notes

QUESTION #107

What are your feelings toward oral sex?

BMW: This is a tricky topic, especially if you are abstaining before marriage, as you should, but Big Mama knows there are all kinds of feelings toward this topic in the secular and religious communities. Do the best you can.

Notes

QUESTION #108

Do you have any sexual addictions and/or disorders?

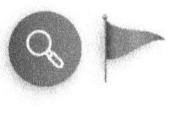

Notes

QUESTION #109

Were you ever in an intimate/sexual relationship with any of my friends prior to our relationship?

Notes

QUESTION #110

> Were you ever in an intimate/sexual relationship with any of my family members prior to our relationship?

Notes

QUESTION #111

Have you been tested for HIV and/or any other sexually transmitted diseases?

Follow-Up: Are you willing to be tested?

Notes

Family Life

Big Mama knows that when you marry the person, you marry the family and the family issues, whether you like it or not. You will not be able to find out everything, but please find out as much as you can so you can make an informed decision about your future in-laws.

QUESTION #112

Tell me about your family history.

Notes

QUESTION #113

How would you describe your relationship with your parents?

Notes

QUESTION #114

Do you want to have children?

BMW: Your answers should match. Don't think you will change his or her mind after you say, "I do."

Notes

QUESTION #115

Do you have a child/children?

BMW: Beware of baby mama/daddy drama.

Notes

QUESTION #116

Where do you want to live and raise a family?

Notes

QUESTION #117

> How soon after marriage do you want to start a family?

Notes

QUESTION #118

Have you been married before?

Notes

QUESTION #119

Are you a momma's boy/daddy's girl?

Notes

QUESTION #120

How is your relationship with your family?

Notes

QUESTION #121

How often do you expect your parents/family to visit?

Notes

QUESTION #122

How will we split time between families during holidays?

Notes

QUESTION #123

Which holidays do you expect to spend with family?

Notes

QUESTION #124

How do you feel about Pets? Do you have Pets?

Notes

QUESTION #125

Do you expect your parents to live with us?

Notes

....
....
....
....
....
....

QUESTION #126

Do you expect us to live with your parents while married?

Notes

QUESTION #127

What is your child-rearing philosophy?

Notes

QUESTION #128

What values are important to you that you plan to instill in your children?

Notes

QUESTION #129

Do you expect your children to be raised by a stay-at-home mother?

Notes

QUESTION #130

What are your beliefs/feelings about child discipline?

Notes

Big Mama Wisdom for Couples | 140

QUESTION #131

How do you handle conflict?

Notes

QUESTION #132

How do you feel about family staying at the house overnight?

Notes

QUESTION #133

Do you share the details of your relationship with family and friends?

Notes

QUESTION #134

Would you consider infertility treatments if we encountered problems becoming pregnant?

Notes

QUESTION #135

In the event we were unable to have children, how do you feel about adoption?

Notes

QUESTION #136

Is infertility a deal-breaker for you?

Notes

Generational Issues

These are extremely sensitive questions; however, they are important topics to discuss when thinking about marriage. If you are unable to discuss these topics openly, Big Mama suggests you consider postponing a wedding until you are able to discuss them openly and honestly.

QUESTION #137

Do you have any genetic diseases in your family?

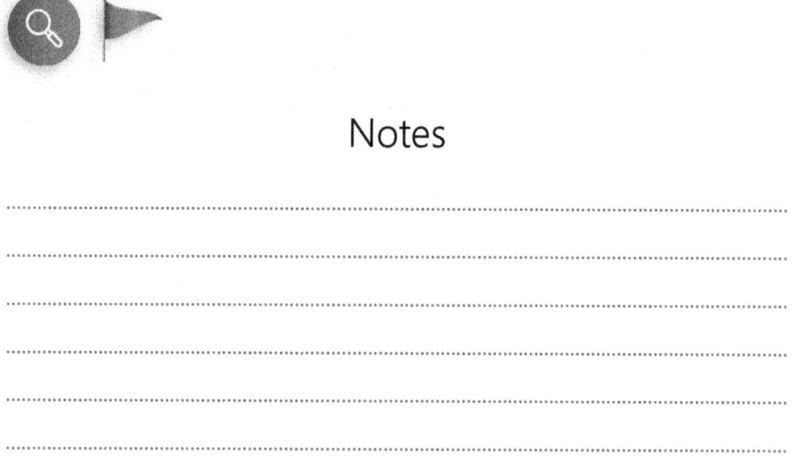

Notes

QUESTION #138

Do you have a family history of mental illness?

Notes

QUESTION #139

Do you have a family history of murder, sociopaths, or psychotic behavior?

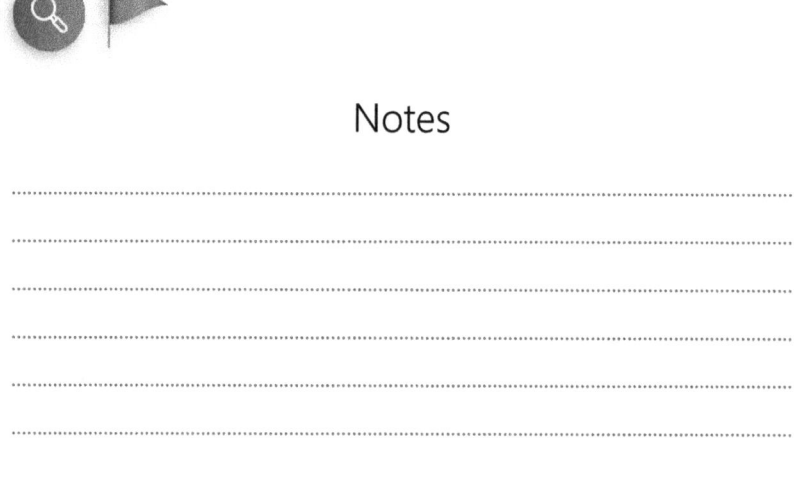

Notes

QUESTION #140

Do you have a family history of incest?

Notes

QUESTION #141

Do you have a family history of alcoholism or drug abuse?

Notes

QUESTION #142

Do you have a family history of domestic violence?

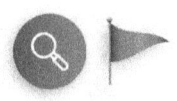

Notes

Social Media

Social Media has become an intricate part of daily life. How everyone manages their social media presence varies. Big Mama knows social media is a volatile issue and needs to be discussed in detail. You should discuss this section carefully. Actively listen to all answers and ask follow up questions when necessary.

QUESTION #143

Do you expect me to give you the password to my phone?

Notes

QUESTION #144

Do you expect to have access to my emails?

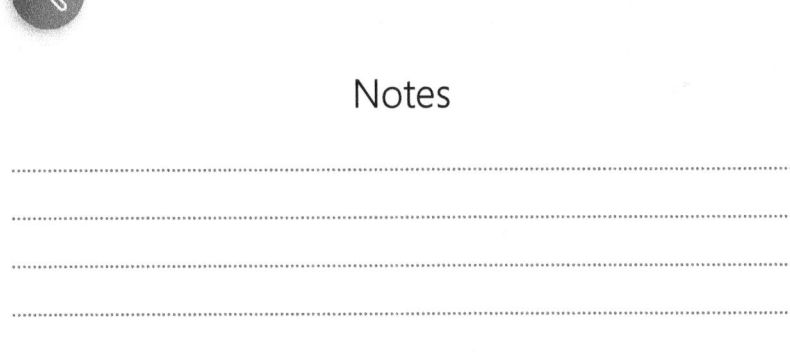

Notes

QUESTION #145

Do you expect to have access to my passwords on Facebook, Twitter, and other social media?

Notes

QUESTION #146

How many hours per week do you spend on social media?

Notes

QUESTION #147

How much of your life do you disclose on social media? Why?

Notes

QUESTION #148

How do you feel about being friends with Exes on social media?

Notes

QUESTION #149

How many social media platforms are you currently active on? Which ones?

Notes

QUESTION #150

Define what trust and privacy means for you on social media. Where are the boundaries?

Notes

QUESTION #151

Do you consider yourself a social media Influencer?

Notes

QUESTION #152

Do you have a social media business?

Notes

QUESTION #153

Do you blog, podcast, YouTube regularly?

Notes

QUESTION #154

Do you have followers? Are followers important to you?

Notes

QUESTION #155

Do you "slide" into people's DM's (direct messages)?

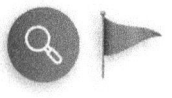

Notes

QUESTION #156

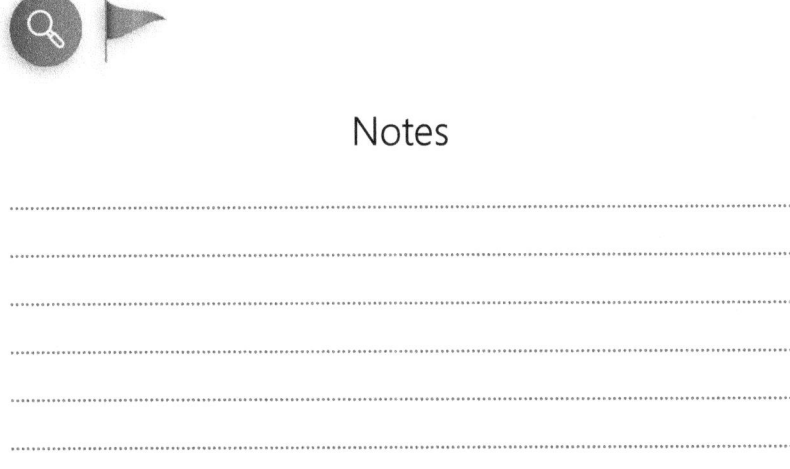

Notes

QUESTION #157

Do you have any social media relationships that may be viewed as "questionable" to a person in a relationship?

Notes

QUESTION #158

Has social media behavior/usage ever been an issue in past relationships?

Notes

QUESTION #159

What do you consider crossing the line on social media when you are in a relationship?

Notes

QUESTION #160

Do you post provocative photos on social media?

Notes

QUESTION #161

Are you willing to openly say you are in a relationship with me on social media? Post photos of us together?

Notes

House & Home

These questions may seem a little bizarre, but Big Mama knows that domestic situations are responsible for the majority of arguments, separations, and divorces. Domicile issues are listed third to money and infidelity as primary reasons for couples' demises.

QUESTION #162

How often do you clean your place?

Notes

QUESTION #163

Do you have a problem with a messy home?

Notes

QUESTION #164

How often do you do laundry?

Notes

QUESTION #165

Do you plan to share in the housekeeping responsibilities?

Notes

QUESTION #166

What are your pet peeves regarding housekeeping?

Notes

QUESTION #167

Which direction do you prefer your toilet paper on the roll?

BMW: Sounds strange, but there are people out there with a specific preference ... and they get hostile about it.

Notes

QUESTION #168

What way do you squeeze your toothpaste?

BMW: Sounds strange, but there are people out there with a specific preference ... and they get hostile about it.

Notes

QUESTION #169

Do you know how to cook?

Notes

QUESTION #170

Do you entertain/party in your home? How often?

Notes

QUESTION #171

How many hours per week do you spend on video games?

Notes

QUESTION #172

How often do you expect to eat at home during the week? Eat out?

Notes

QUESTION #173

Do you make your bed every morning when you get up?

Notes

QUESTION #174

How many hours per week do you dedicate to your social activities/sporting events/clubs/memberships?

Notes

Personal Issues

These are extremely sensitive questions; however, they are important topics to discuss when thinking about marriage. If you are unable to discuss these topics openly, Big Mama suggests you consider postponing a wedding until you are able to discuss them openly and honestly.

Big Mama Wisdom for Couples | 189

QUESTION #175

Are you a jealous person?

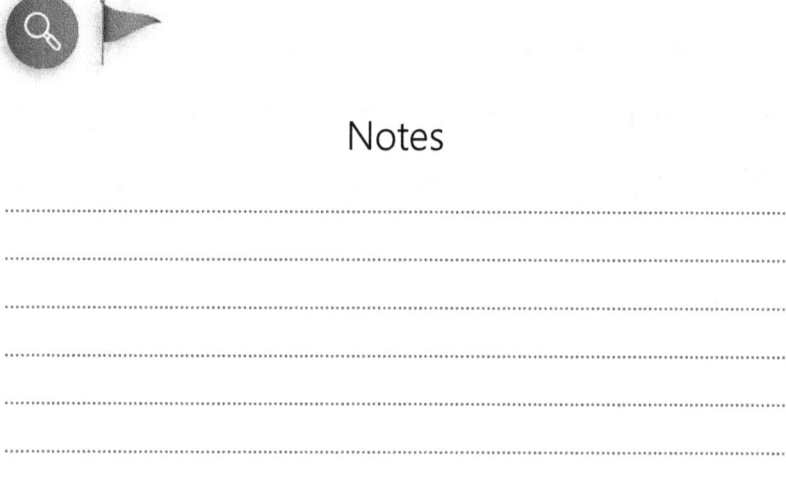

Notes

QUESTION #176

Do you have any allergies?

Notes

QUESTION #177

Do you have any medical issues?

Notes

QUESTION #178

Are you managing or undergoing treatment for a sexually transmitted disease?

Notes

QUESTION #179

What are your thoughts on vaccinations in general?

Notes

QUESTION #180

Did you receive the Covid-19 vaccine? Are you okay if I did not?

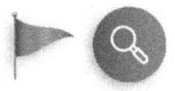

Notes

QUESTION #181

Have you experienced any type of abuse in your lifetime?

Notes

QUESTION #182

Have you experienced any type of trauma or had a traumatic experience in your life?

Notes

QUESTION #183

What are your thoughts on therapy? Are you currently in treatment?

Notes

QUESTION #184

What bad habits do you currently have that you would like to break?

Notes

QUESTION #185

Do you participate in recreational drugs?

Notes

QUESTION #186

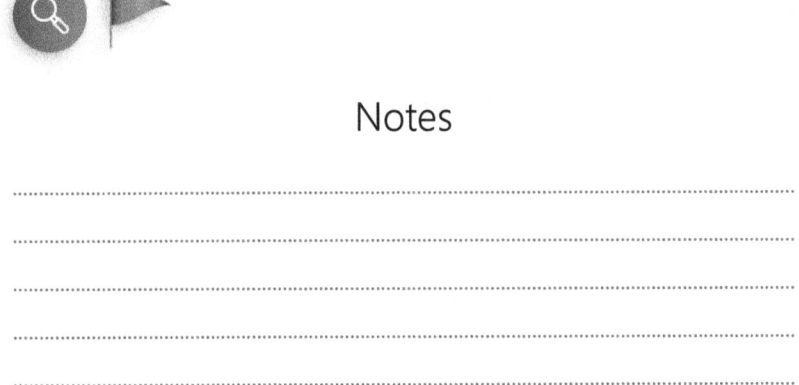

Notes

QUESTION #187

Are you an alcoholic or a recovering alcoholic?

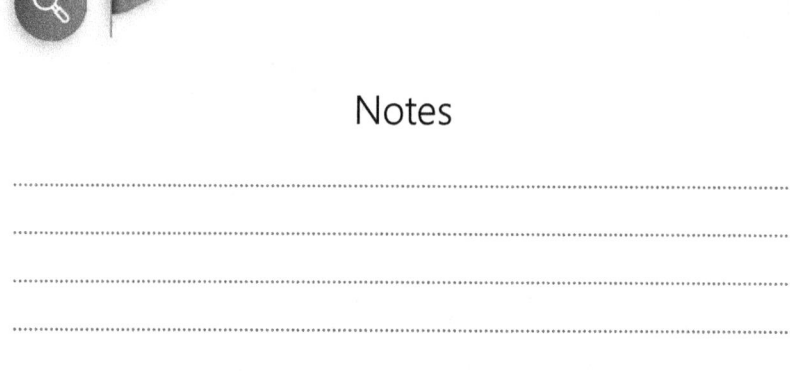

Notes

QUESTION #188

Have you ever been incarcerated?

Notes

QUESTION #189

Are you on probation?

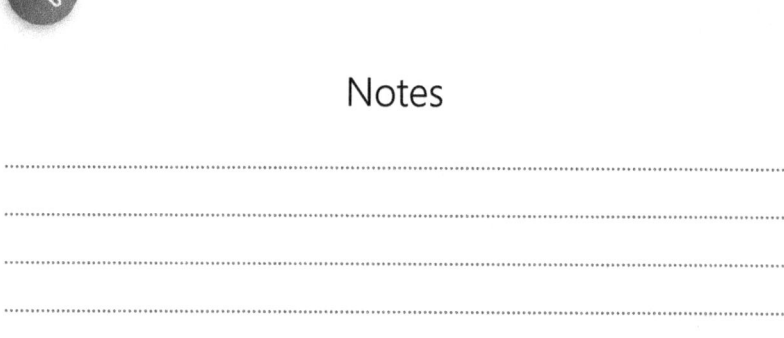

Notes

QUESTION #190

Do you have a gambling addiction?

Notes

QUESTION #191

Do you know your drinking limit?

Notes

QUESTION #192

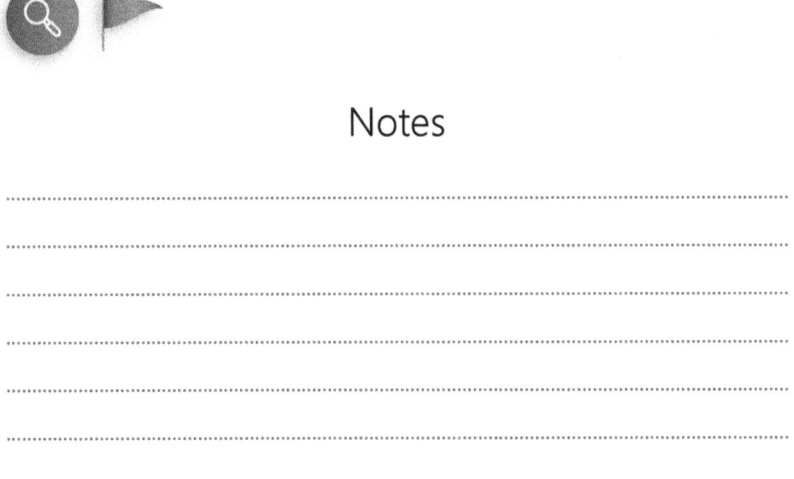

Notes

QUESTION #193

Have you ever struggled with depression?

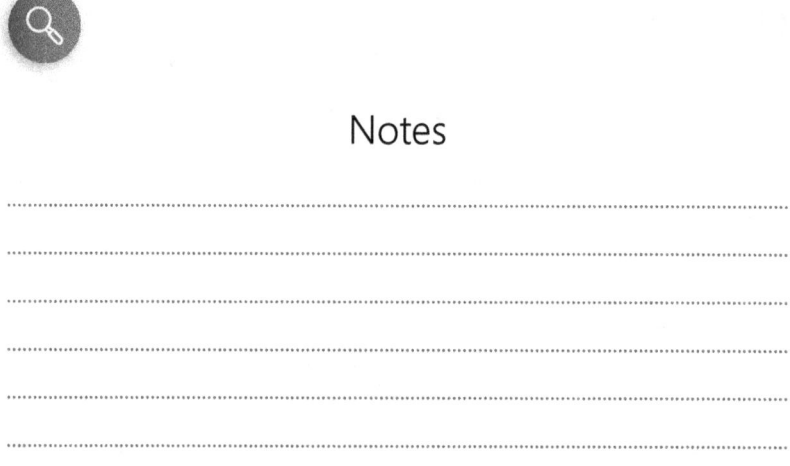

Notes

QUESTION #194

Do you look at or purchase pornography?

Notes

QUESTION #195

Do you have any fetishes?

Notes

QUESTION #196

Have you ever hit your partner?

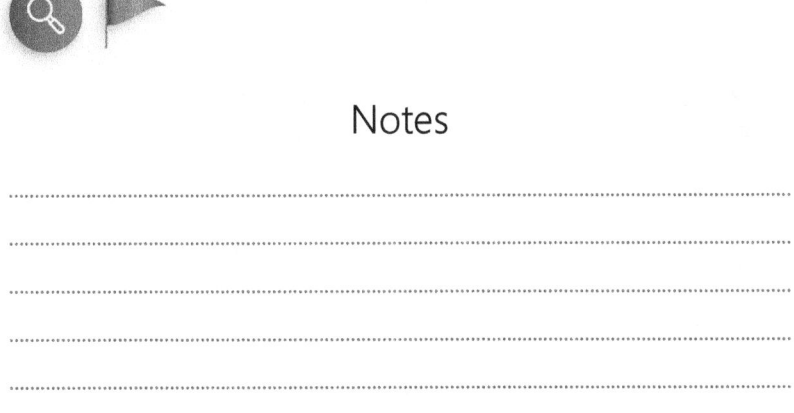

Notes

QUESTION #197

Have you ever been involved in any domestic violence situations?

Notes

QUESTION #198

Do you own a gun? If so, is it registered? Do you have a license to carry a weapon?

BMW: You should feel comfortable with the answers.

Notes

QUESTION #199

Should I be worried about any of your ex-partners? Why?

Notes

QUESTION #200

Do you currently or have you ever had an exparte or restraining order placed on you?

Notes

QUESTION #201

What are the stories behind your tattoos and piercings?

Notes

QUESTION #202

Do you go out to clubs/bars on a regular basis?

Follow-Up: Do you expect to continue clubbing/going to bars after we get married?

Notes

QUESTION #203

Do you drink and drive?

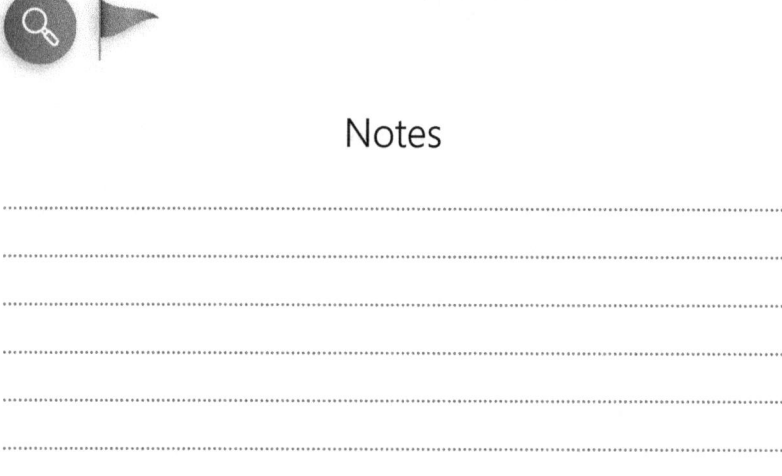

Notes

QUESTION #204

What are your views on race and race relations?

Notes

QUESTION #205

What information, if discovered, would make you end a relationship immediately?

Notes

References

eHarmony Staff, *15 Great First Date Questions*, no date provided, <http://www.eharmony.com/dating-advice/dating/15-great-first-date-questions/> (May, 2012)

180 questions to ask your boyfriend. (2020, November 18). The Nest - The Nest. https://www.thenest.com/content/questions-to-ask-your-boyfriend

Garcia, G. (2020, March 20). *50 questions for couples to get to know each other better.* The Cut. https://www.google.com/amp/s/www.thecut.com/amp/article/questions-for-couples.html

About The Author

Cynthia Knight married her childhood sweetheart twenty-nine years ago. From this union she has two adult children and resides with her husband in the suburbs of Baltimore, Maryland. She is described by friends and family as an "old soul." In her spare time Cynthia likes to crochet, cook, and entertain.

For book signings, speaking engagements, and general information contact: bookings@onyxgavel.com

www.ingramcontent.com/pod-product-compliance
Lightning Source LLC
Chambersburg PA
CBHW071909290426
44110CB00013B/1328